I0503156

SEXUAL HARASSMENT: WORKPLACE ISSUES
(TRAINING WORKBOOK)

© Copyright 2008 David Peterson Harvey
and Gloria Stevenson

TABLE OF CONTENTS

TRAINEE MATERIALS

The training materials in this book were designed to serve as companion materials to the "Sexual Harassment: Workplace Issues" training videos available from thehiddenart.com. They can also be used as standalone training materials or in conjunction with other sexual harassment training programs, providing the trainer with a broad range of opportunities.

The overview gives a broad definition of sexual harassment, outlines a company's basic responsibilities, and lists the basic protections for anyone who makes a report or inquiry regarding sexual harassment. It is followed by a list of questions designed to test your basic understanding. Following the overview section are descriptions of the sexual harassment scenarios presented in the training videos and questions designed to test your knowledge of sexual harassment as it relates to each scenario.

As you work through the problems in this book, keep in mind that the key factors in avoiding harassment and discrimination are developing an understanding of, balancing and being sensitive to the feelings of the people around you. By avoiding harassment and discrimination of all types in your work, you become a more valuable employee or contractor as you help create a more trusting and productive work environment.

OVERVIEW

Organizations have a clear responsibility to establish sexual harassment policies, train their employees on these policies, investigate any reports of sexual harassment and to enforce these policies to eliminate sexual harassment from the workplace.

Sexual harassment is a violation of Title VII of the Civil Rights Act of 1964, and it can involve the behavior of a person of either sex against a person of either the opposite sex or the same sex. It occurs when the behavior constitutes unwelcome sexual advances, unwelcome requests for sexual favors, and other unwelcome verbal or physical behavior of a sexual nature.

Companies should provide a clear chain of command and procedures for dealing with issues involving possible sexual harassment, including dealing with malicious or false accusations, counseling and informal resolution and formal complaint resolution.

If you are aware of or have experienced an incident of sexual harassment, report it promptly to the person in the company who handles inquiries or complaints about sexual harassment. Remember, no one may be subjected to restraint, interference, coercion or reprisal for action taken in good faith to seek advice concerning a sexual harassment matter, to file a sexual harassment complaint or to serve as a witness or a panel member in the investigation of a sexual harassment complaint.

QUESTION & ANSWER

Question: Can I lose my job because I refuse to go on a date with someone? Also, what if I complain? Can I lose my job for complaining?

Answer:

_____

Question: Is giving a hug or a kiss to your coworker considered sexual harassment if they don't feel they are being harassed?

Answer:

_____

Question: Do I have the right to keep suggestive pictures in my office? What about sending dirty jokes or other suggestive materials through email?

Answer:

_____

Question: I know sexual jokes are inappropriate, but what about showing appreciation of how good someone looks? I mean, you don't even have to say anything; you can gesture or whistle or something. Is that okay?

Answer:

_____

Question: What about bumping into someone or blocking their way? Can physical contact of this sort be considered sexual harassment?

Answer:

_____

TROUBLE AT THE WATER COOLER

Don Lucas stands near the water cooler with papers in his hands, talking to Ryan Wensley, when Tina Sokolova walks by them. Tina is wearing a short dress. Ryan looks her up and down appreciatively.

Ryan: (in a cheesy, suggestive voice) Hello, sweetheart! How did you sleep last night?

Both men stare at her legs as she walks past. She turns away from them and walks away. Don whistles at her.

QUESTIONS:

1. Which actions in this scenario represent sexual harassment?

    a. The way both men look at Tina.

    b. Ryan's tone of voice.

    c. Ryan calling Tina "sweetheart."

    d. Ryan's question about how Tina slept.

    e. All of the above.

Answer:

_____

2. What could Tina have done to better handle the situation?

   a. Appreciate the fact that both men found her attractive.

   b. Flirt back since it was all harmless fun.

   c. Wiggle her hips when she walked away.

   d. Told them to stop acting this way toward her.

   e. Answers a, b, and c.

Answer:

_____

3. When is flirting like this considered sexual harassment?

   a. The person receiving the attention doesn't like it.

   b. A third party views it as inappropriate.

   c. Only if all parties involved decide it's not appropriate.

   d. The person receiving the attention asks that it be stopped.

   e. Answers a, b, and d.

Answer:

_____

© 2008 David Peterson Harvey and Gloria Stevenson

MORNING MEETING GONE WRONG

Tina Sokolova, Don Lucas and Ryan Wensley have just finished a meeting in the conference room. Tina moves to leave the room and Ryan blocks her way. He touches her to get her attention. Don stands watching with amusement.

Ryan: Hey, you look great today! What do you say we go out after work and have some fun, just you and me?

Tina: No thank you.

Ryan: I think we make great partners at work. I just thought we should get to know each other a little better. You don't want me to tell the boss about you being unfriendly to work with, do you?

Tina pushes past him and leaves the room.

QUESTIONS:

4. Which of Ryan's actions in this scenario represent sexual harassment?

    a. Blocking Tina's way and touching her.

    b. Asking Tina out on a date.

    c. Threatening to tell the boss she was unfriendly.

    d. Answers a and c.

    e. Answers a, b and c.

Answer:

5. Is asking someone on a date at work sexual harassment?

    a. Yes; you should never date a coworker.

    b. It is if you ask again after being turned down the first time.

    c. It is if you suggest it will threaten the other person's work environment.

    d. It is if someone else feels it creates an unfair work environment for them.

    e. Answers b, c and d.

Answer:

_____

RYAN'S CUBICLE

Ryan Wensley is at his desk working. Dominique Duncan comes into his cubicle and sits on his desk suggestively with her legs exposed.

Dominique: Hi, sweetie! Are those reports finished yet?

Ryan: (trying to ignore her while working) I'm almost finished.

Dominique: Oh, you're so tense. I think you need to relax. (walks behind him and massages his shoulders) Boy, you are tense!

Ryan: Cut it out, Dominique!

Dominique: (giggles) You're so strong and firm! (sighs when he doesn't respond) Okay, just get me that report.

QUESTIONS:

6. Was Dominique calling Ryan sweetie sexual harassment?

    a. No. She was merely trying to be nice.

    b. Yes. You should never call someone that at work.

    c. It could be if he was offended by it.

    d. No. It is all right to harass someone who harasses other people.

    e. Both a and d.

Answer:
_____

7. What else about this scenario could be considered sexual harassment?

   a. Comments about him being strong and firm.

   b. The way she sat at his desk.

   c. The unwelcome physical contact.

   d. The outfit she was wearing.

   e. Answers a, b, and c.

Answer:

_____

DOMINIQUE'S CUBICLE

Dominique Duncan sits in her cubicle and opens a birthday card with a cartoon of a male stripper on it. She opens the birthday card. Hand written inside is, "No real man can satisfy you. Or maybe you just haven't found the right one. Happy Birthday, Don."

She throws the card across the desk in disgust. Tina Sokolova enters the room and sees her expression.

Tina: Dominique, what's wrong?

Dominique: Nothing.

Tina picks up the pieces of the card and reads it.

Tina: Men are such dogs!

Tina hugs Dominique and looks like she is really enjoying it. Dominique pushes her away.

Dominique: Look, thanks but no thanks.

QUESTIONS:

8. What observations can you make about this scene?

    a. Tina saying that men are dogs could be considered sexual harassment.

    b. Tina hugging Dominique could be considered sexual harassment.

    c. It's not sexual harassment when it involves two women.

    d. Don's card would have been appropriate if it came from another woman.

    e. Both a and b are true.

Answer:

_____

9. What else about this scenario could be considered sexual harassment?

    a. Don's birthday card.

    b. The way Tina walked into the room.

    c. Tina reading the birthday card without asking.

    d. The outfit Tina was wearing.

    e. Answers a, b and d.

Answer:

THE PROBLEM WITH COFFEE

Ryan Wensley is drinking coffee with Don Lucas when Dominique Duncan enters the coffee room. She blows a kiss at Ryan, who ignores her.

Dominique: He doesn't like me. I think he's gay.

Don: (slaps Ryan on the butt, causing him to choke on his coffee) Oh, no, honey; he's not gay. I think he just doesn't like anybody.

Dominique: Look, thanks but no thanks.

QUESTIONS:

10. When Don slapped Ryan, could it be considered sexual harassment?

    a.   No. Neither of the men were gay.

    b.   Yes. Don seems a little gay.

    c.   No. The two men are friends, so it's okay to joke around like that.

    d.   Yes. It doesn't matter whether either man is gay.

    e.   Both a and c are true.

Answer:

_____

11. What else about this scenario could be considered sexual harassment?

   a. Dominique blowing the kiss.

   b. Ryan gulping his coffee.

   c. The suggestive way the men were standing in the scene.

   d. Dominique suggesting that Ryan was gay.

   e. Both a and d are true.

Answer:

_____

NOTE: In some cases, unwelcome physical contact (such as being slapped on the rear), or even the anticipation of unwelcome contact can be considered physical or sexual assault and/or battery. In cases where physical contact occurs, the victim may be able to file criminal charges and civil action against the assailant.

TRAINER MATERIALS

The training materials in this book were designed to serve as companion materials to the "Sexual Harassment: Workplace Issues" training videos available from thehiddenart.com. They can also be used as standalone training materials or in conjunction with other sexual harassment training programs, providing you with a broad range of training opportunities.

The overview gives a broad definition of sexual harassment, outlines a company's basic responsibilities, and lists the basic protections for anyone who makes a report or inquiry regarding sexual harassment. It is followed by a list of questions designed to test the trainee's basic understanding. Following the overview section are descriptions of the sexual harassment scenarios presented in the training videos and questions designed to test the trainee's knowledge of sexual harassment as it relates to each scenario.

As the trainee follows your presentation and works through the problems in this book, it is important to stress that the key factors in avoiding harassment and discrimination are developing an understanding of, balancing and being sensitive to the feelings of the people around you. The trainee should be shown that, by avoiding harassment and discrimination of all types in the workplace, he or she becomes a more valuable asset to the company as he or she helps create a more trusting and productive work environment.

OVERVIEW

Organizations have a clear responsibility to establish sexual harassment policies, train their employees on these policies, investigate any reports of sexual harassment and to enforce these policies to eliminate sexual harassment from the workplace.

Sexual harassment is a violation of Title VII of the Civil Rights Act of 1964, and it can involve the behavior of a person of either sex against a person of either the opposite sex or the same sex. It occurs when the behavior constitutes unwelcome sexual advances, unwelcome requests for sexual favors, and other unwelcome verbal or physical behavior of a sexual nature.

Companies should provide a clear chain of command and procedures for dealing with issues involving possible sexual harassment, including dealing with malicious or false accusations, counseling and informal resolution and formal complaint resolution.

If you are aware of or have experienced an incident of sexual harassment, report it promptly to the person in the company who handles inquiries or complaints about sexual harassment. Remember, no one may be subjected to restraint, interference, coercion or reprisal for action taken in good faith to seek advice concerning a sexual harassment matter, to file a sexual harassment complaint or to serve as a witness or a panel member in the investigation of a sexual harassment complaint.

QUESTION & ANSWER

Question: Can I lose my job because I refuse to go on a date with someone? Also, what if I complain? Can I lose my job for complaining?

Answer: No one may threaten or insinuate that your employment, wages, promotions, work assignments or other employment conditions may be adversely affected by not submitting to sexual advances. Also, no company may fire you for filing a legitimate complaint or for asking for information concerning sexual harassment.

Question: Is giving a hug or a kiss to your coworker considered sexual harassment if they don't feel they are being harassed?

Answer: The problem is that in the office the behavior is not just between you and a coworker. If someone else is offended by the behavior, or if they think that someone is receiving special treatment because of the relationship, it could be considered sexual harassment.

Question: Do I have the right to keep suggestive pictures in my office? What about sending dirty jokes or other suggestive materials through email?

Answer: Even if it is in your private office, you may not keep sexually suggestive objects, pictures, videotapes, audio recordings or literature that may embarrass or offend someone else. Also, you may not send others material of a suggestive nature to anyone in any form, including phone messages, faxes or any form of Internet delivery.

Question: I know sexual jokes are inappropriate, but what about showing appreciation of how good someone looks? I mean, you don't even have to say anything; you can gesture or whistle or something. Is that okay?

Answer: Unwelcome verbal expressions of a sexual nature, including graphic sexual commentaries about a person's body, dress, appearance, or sexual activities, the unwelcome use of sexually degrading language, jokes, innuendoes, unwelcome suggestive or insulting sounds or whistles can be considered sexual harassment. This can include gestures as well.

Question: What about bumping into someone or blocking their way? Can physical contact of this sort be considered sexual harassment?

Answer: If the actions are intentional, they can be considered sexual harassment. Two of the key guiding factors in this are whether the incidents are isolated or repeated and whether the person receiving the physical contact perceives the contact as threatening or harassing in nature.

TROUBLE AT THE WATER COOLER

Don Lucas stands near the water cooler with papers in his hands, talking to Ryan Wensley, when Tina Sokolova walks by them. Tina is wearing a short dress. Ryan looks her up and down appreciatively.

Ryan: (in a cheesy, suggestive voice) Hello, sweetheart! How did you sleep last night?

Both men stare at her legs as she walks past. She turns away from them and walks away. Don whistles at her.

QUESTIONS:

1. Which actions in this scenario represent sexual harassment?

    a. The way both men look at Tina.

    b. Ryan's tone of voice.

    c. Ryan calling Tina "sweetheart."

    d. Ryan's question about how Tina slept.

    e. All of the above.

Answer: e. All of the above.

2. What could Tina have done to better handle the situation?

    a. Appreciate the fact that both men found her attractive.

    b. Flirt back since it was all harmless fun.

    c. Wiggle her hips when she walked away.

    d. Told them to stop acting this way toward her.

    e. Answers a, b, and c.

Answer: d. Told them to stop acting this way toward her.

3. When is flirting like this considered sexual harassment?

   a. The person receiving the attention doesn't like it.

   b. A third party views it as inappropriate.

   c. Only if all parties involved decide it's not appropriate.

   d. The person receiving the attention asks that it be stopped.

   e. Answers a, b, and d.

Answer: e. Answers a, b and d.

MORNING MEETING GONE WRONG

Tina Sokolova, Don Lucas and Ryan Wensley have just finished a meeting in the conference room. Tina moves to leave the room and Ryan blocks her way. He touches her to get her attention. Don stands watching with amusement.

Ryan: Hey, you look great today! What do you say we go out after work and have some fun, just you and me?

Tina: No thank you.

Ryan: I think we make great partners at work. I just thought we should get to know each other a little better. You don't want me to tell the boss about you being unfriendly to work with, do you?

Tina pushes past him and leaves the room.

QUESTIONS:

4. Which of Ryan's actions in this scenario represent sexual harassment?

    a. Blocking Tina's way and touching her.

    b. Asking Tina out on a date.

    c. Threatening to tell the boss she was unfriendly.

    d. Answers a and c.

    e. Answers a, b and c.

Answer: d. Answers a and c.

5. Is asking someone on a date at work sexual harassment?

   a. Yes; you should never date a coworker.

   b. It is if you ask again after being turned down the first time.

   c. It is if you suggest it will threaten the other person's work environment.

   d. It is if someone else feels it creates an unfair work environment for them.

   e. Answers b, c and d.

Answer: e. Answers b, c and d.

RYAN'S CUBICLE

Ryan Wensley is at his desk working. Dominique Duncan comes into his cubicle and sits on his desk suggestively with her legs exposed.

Dominique: Hi, sweetie! Are those reports finished yet?

Ryan: (trying to ignore her while working) I'm almost finished.

Dominique: Oh, you're so tense. I think you need to relax. (walks behind him and massages his shoulders) Boy, you are tense!

Ryan: Cut it out, Dominique!

Dominique: (giggles) You're so strong and firm! (sighs when he doesn't respond) Okay, just get me that report.

QUESTIONS:

6. Was Dominique calling Ryan sweetie sexual harassment?

    a. No. She was merely trying to be nice.

    b. Yes. You should never call someone that at work.

    c. It could be if he was offended by it.

    d. No. It is all right to harass someone who harasses other people.

    e. Both a and d.

Answer: c. It could be if he was offended by it.

7. What else about this scenario could be considered sexual harassment?

   a. Comments about him being strong and firm.

   b. The way she sat at his desk.

   c. The unwelcome physical contact.

   d. The outfit she was wearing.

   e. Answers a, b, and c.

Answer: e. Answers a, b and c.

DOMINIQUE'S CUBICLE

Dominique Duncan sits in her cubicle and opens a birthday card with a cartoon of a male stripper on it. She opens the birthday card. Hand written inside is, "No real man can satisfy you. Or maybe you just haven't found the right one. Happy Birthday, Don."

She throws the card across the desk in disgust. Tina Sokolova enters the room and sees her expression.

Tina: Dominique, what's wrong?

Dominique: Nothing.

Tina picks up the pieces of the card and reads it.

Tina: Men are such dogs!

Tina hugs Dominique and looks like she is really enjoying it. Dominique pushes her away.

Dominique: Look, thanks but no thanks.

QUESTIONS:

8. What observations can you make about this scene?

    a. Tina saying that men are dogs could be considered sexual harassment.

    b. Tina hugging Dominique could be considered sexual harassment.

    c. It's not sexual harassment when it involves two women.

    d. Don's card would have been appropriate if it came from another woman.

    e. Both a and b are true.

Answer: e. Both a and b are true.

9. What else about this scenario could be considered sexual harassment?

   a. Don's birthday card.

   b. The way Tina walked into the room.

   c. Tina reading the birthday card without asking.

   d. The outfit Tina was wearing.

   e. Answers a, b and d.

Answer: a. Don's birthday card.

THE PROBLEM WITH COFFEE

Ryan Wensley is drinking coffee with Don Lucas when Dominique Duncan enters the coffee room. She blows a kiss at Ryan, who ignores her.

Dominique: He doesn't like me. I think he's gay.

Don: (slaps Ryan on the butt, causing him to choke on his coffee) Oh, no, honey; he's not gay. I think he just doesn't like anybody.

Dominique: Look, thanks but no thanks.

QUESTIONS:

10. When Don slapped Ryan, could it be considered sexual harassment?

    a. No. Neither of the men were gay.

    b. Yes. Don seems a little gay.

    c. No. The two men are friends, so it's okay to joke around like that.

    d. Yes. It doesn't matter whether either man is gay.

    e. Both a and c are true.

Answer: d. Yes. It doesn't matter whether either man is gay.

11. What else about this scenario could be considered sexual harassment?

   a. Dominique blowing the kiss.

   b. Ryan gulping his coffee.

   c. The suggestive way the men were standing in the scene.

   d. Dominique suggesting that Ryan was gay.

   e. Both a and d are true.

Answer: e. Both a and d are true.

NOTE: In some cases, unwelcome physical contact (such as being slapped on the rear), or even the anticipation of unwelcome contact can be considered physical or sexual assault and/or battery. In cases where physical contact occurs, the victim may be able to file criminal charges and civil action against the assailant.

www.ingramcontent.com/pod-product-compliance
Lightning Source LLC
Chambersburg PA
CBHW051420170526
45165CB00004BA/1892